W9-CDO-512

MORE SUPER
SIMPLE SCIENCE

SCIENCE EXPERIMENTS WITH

# FOOD

A Division of ABDO
**ABDO**
Publishing Company

BY ALEX KUSKOWSKI          Consulting Editor, Diane Craig, M.A./Reading Specialist

# visit us at www.abdopublishing.com

Published by ABDO Publishing Company, a division of ABDO, P.O. Box 398166, Minneapolis, Minnesota 55439. Copyright © 2014 by Abdo Consulting Group, Inc. International copyrights reserved in all countries. No part of this book may be reproduced in any form without written permission from the publisher. Super SandCastle™ is a trademark and logo of ABDO Publishing Company.

Printed in the United States of America, North Mankato, Minnesota
062013
112013

 PRINTED ON RECYCLED PAPER

Editor: Liz Salzmann
Content Developer: Alex Kuskowski
Cover and Interior Design and Production: Mighty Media, Inc.
Photo Credits: Aaron DeYoe, Shutterstock

The following manufacturers/names appearing in this book are trademarks:
Arm & Hammer®, C&H®, Crystal Sugar®, Gedney®, Gefen®, Karo®, Land O Lakes®, Market Pantry™, McCormick®, Mod Podge®, Morton®, Pyrex®, Roundy's®, Stanley®, Sunbeam®

**Library of Congress Cataloging-in-Publication Data**
Kuskowski, Alex.
  Science Experiments with food / by Alex Kuskowski ; consulting editor, Diane Craig.
    p. cm. -- (More super simple science)
  Audience: 005-010.
  ISBN 978-1-61783-849-1
  1. Food--Experiments--Juvenile literature. 2. Science--Methodology--Juvenile literature. I. Craig, Diane. II. Title.
  TX355.K87 2014
  641.5'083--dc23
                    2012049827

Super SandCastle™ books are created by a team of professional educators, reading specialists, and content developers around five essential components—phonemic awareness, phonics, vocabulary, text comprehension, and fluency—to assist young readers as they develop reading skills and strategies and increase their general knowledge. All books are written, reviewed, and leveled for guided reading, early reading intervention, and Accelerated Reader® programs for use in shared, guided, and independent reading and writing activities to support a balanced approach to literacy instruction.

## TO ADULT HELPERS

Learning about science is fun and simple to do. There are just a few things to remember to keep kids safe. Some activities in this book recommend adult supervision. Be sure to review the activities before starting, and be ready to assist your budding scientist when necessary.

## KEY SYMBOLS

Look for these symbols in this book.

**SHARP!**
You will be working with a sharp object. Get help!

**HOT!**
You will be working with something hot. Get help!

# TABLE OF CONTENTS

# SUPER SIMPLE SCIENCE

You can be a scientist! It's super simple. Science is all around you. Learning about the world around you is part of the fun of science. Science is in your house, your backyard, and on the playground.

Find science in lemons and milk. Look for science in butter or blackberries. Try the activities in this book. You'll never know where to find science unless you look!

## SCIENCE WITH FOOD

Use food to learn about science. Science explains how ice cream is made, and why a lemon can power a light. In this book you will see how all kinds of foods can help you learn about science.

# WORK LIKE A SCIENTIST

Scientists have a special way of working. It is a series of steps called the Scientific Method. Follow the steps to work like a scientist.

**1** Look at something. What do you see? What does it do?

**2** Think of a question about the thing you are watching. What is it like? Why is it like that? How did it get that way?

**3** Think of a possible answer to the question.

**4** Do a test to find out if you are right. Write down what happened.

**5** Think about it. Were you right? Why or why not?

## KEEP TRACK

There's another way to be just like a scientist. Scientists make notes about everything they do. Get a notebook. When you do an experiment, write down what happens in each step. It's super simple!

# WHAT YOU WILL NEED

14-gram, coated copper wire & alligator clips

angel hair pasta

baking sheet

baking soda

blackberries

candy thermometer

corn syrup

cotton swab

dinner knife & spoon

duct tape

felt, googly eyes & glitter (optional)

food coloring

glass jar

granulated & powdered sugar

heavy whipping cream & whole milk

large ionized nails

lemons & lemon juice

liquid dish soap

**measuring cups
& spoons**

**mint & vanilla
extract**

**mixing bowls
& spoon**

**Mod Podge**

**paintbrush**

**pennies**

**plastic cup &
drinking glass**

**plastic zipper
bags**

**plate**

**pliers & wire
stripper**

**rolling pin**

**ruler**

**saucepans
& oven mitts**

**sharp knife
& cutting board**

**small candy mold**

**small LED light**

**strainer**

**table salt, sour
salt & rock salt**

**waxed paper**

**white vinegar**

# MILK & COLOR EXPLOSION

## WHAT YOU WILL NEED

liquid dish soap

plastic cup

plate

whole milk

red, yellow, & blue food coloring

cotton swab

## DIRECTIONS

1   Put some dish soap in a plastic cup.

②   Pour milk onto the plate. Completely cover the bottom.

③   Put a few drops of food coloring in the milk. Use all of the colors. Put the drops in the same spot.

④   Dip a cotton swab in the soap. Then touch it to the spot of food coloring. Don't move the cotton swab. Watch what happens!

## WHAT'S GOING ON?

Milk has fats in it. The soap causes the fats in the milk to move. The food coloring shows how the soap pushes the fats around.

# BERRY BASE, BERRY ACID

## WHAT YOU WILL NEED

½ cup blackberries

plastic zipper bag

¾ cup water

measuring cups & spoons

medium bowl

3 strips of paper

paper towels

3 plastic cups

1 teaspoon baking soda

¼ cup lemon juice

Find out what is basic and what is **acidic**!

# DIRECTIONS PART 1

1. Put the berries in the plastic bag. Zip the bag closed. Smash the bag with your fingers until the fruit looks like jam.

2. Add ¼ cup water to the bag. Zip up the bag and mix well. Pour the mixture into a bowl.

3. Soak the strips of paper in the berry juice.

4. Take out the paper strips. Pull them between your thumb and finger. This removes the extra juice. Lay them flat on a paper towel to dry.

# DIRECTIONS PART 2

⑤ Line up three cups. Put ¼ cup water in the first cup. Put ¼ cup lemon juice in the second cup.

⑥ Put the baking soda and ¼ cup of water in the third cup. Stir it with a spoon.

⑦ Dip half of one strip in each cup. Lay them on a paper towel to dry. Each of the strips should be a different color.

## WHAT'S GOING ON?

Lemon juice is an **acid**. It turns blackberry paper red. The baking soda is a **base**. It turns blackberry paper blue. Water is **neutral**. The blackberry paper doesn't change color.

# 03 SWEET & SOUR ROCK CANDY

## WHAT YOU WILL NEED

baking sheet
measuring cups & spoons
1 cup powdered sugar
6 tablespoons sour salt
2 cups granulated sugar
¼ cup water
⅓ cup corn syrup
medium saucepan
mixing spoon
candy thermometer
¼ teaspoon mint extract
1 teaspoon baking soda
3 drops green food coloring
1-quart plastic zipper bag
rolling pin

# DIRECTIONS PART 1

① Put the powdered sugar in the baking sheet. Spread it in an even layer. Sprinkle 3 tablespoons of sour salt over the sugar.

② Put the granulated sugar, water, and corn syrup in a saucepan. Put it on the stove over **medium** heat. Stir gently.

③ Heat the pan until the mixture begins to bubble. Then hold the candy thermometer in the pan. Continue stirring. Watch for the thermometer to read 305 **degrees**. Remove the pan from the heat.

# DIRECTIONS PART 2

④ Wait for the thermometer to read 275 **degrees**. Quickly add the mint extract, baking soda, and food coloring. Stir.

⑤ Pour the mixture onto the cookie sheet. Have an adult help you.

6 Sprinkle the remaining sour salt on top. Let it cool completely. Then put it in a plastic bag.

⑦ Use a rolling pin to crush the candy into small pieces. Have a taste of your sweet and sour treat!

## WHAT'S GOING ON?

Heating sugar and water to 305 degrees causes the water to boil away. All that's left is hot sugar. When it cools, it turns into sugar rocks.

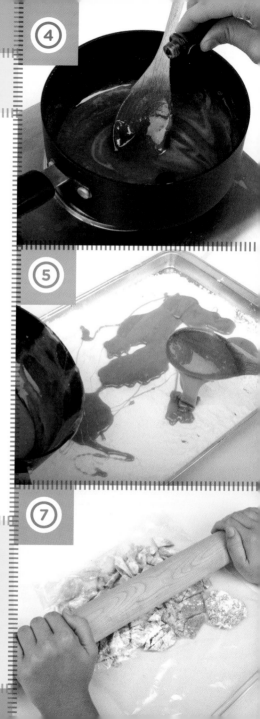

# SHAKE-IT-UP ICE CREAM

## WHAT YOU WILL NEED

½ cup whole milk

½ cup heavy whipping cream

¼ cup granulated sugar

¼ tablespoon vanilla extract

measuring cups & spoons

1-quart plastic zipper bag

1-gallon plastic zipper bag

duct tape

2 cups ice

½ cup rock salt

oven mitts

# DIRECTIONS

① Put the milk, whipping cream, sugar, and vanilla in the one-quart plastic bag. Seal the bag. Put tape over the opening of the bag.

2  Put the ice and rock salt in the gallon plastic bag.

③ Put the quart plastic bag inside the gallon plastic bag. Seal the bag.

④ Put on oven mitts. Pick up the bags. Shake them for 10 minutes.

5  Open the bag and take out the quart bag. Take off the tape. Open the bag. You made ice cream!

## WHAT'S GOING ON?

Salt lowers the temperature at which ice melts. By adding salt, the ice becomes colder. The cream is chilled by the very cold ice and becomes ice cream.

# 05 HOMEMADE LEMON SODA

## WHAT YOU WILL NEED

2 lemons

sharp knife

cutting board

measuring cup

drinking glass

½ cup water

spoon

½ cup granulated sugar

1 teaspoon baking soda

# DIRECTIONS

1    Cut the lemons in half.

②    **Squeeze** the lemon juice into the measuring cup. Remove the seeds.

③    Put ½ cup of lemon juice in the glass. Add the water. Stir.

4    Stir in the sugar.

⑤    Add the baking soda. Take a drink of your **fizzy** lemon soda!

## WHAT'S GOING ON?

Baking soda is a type of salt called sodium bicarbonate. Lemon juice has **acid** in it. Mixing them creates **carbon dioxide** bubbles. That makes the drink fizzy!

# SCIENTIFIC BUTTER SPREAD

market pantry™

original

## WHAT YOU WILL NEED

1½ cup heavy whipping cream

measuring cups

glass jar with lid

strainer

bowl

½ cup water

salt

# DIRECTIONS

1 Take the cream out of the refrigerator. Leave it out for 9 hours.

2 Pour the cream into the jar. Put on the lid. Hold the jar with both hands. Shake for 3 minutes.

3 Open the jar. Use the strainer to remove the extra liquid. Leave the rest in the jar.

4 Put the water in the jar. Put the lid back on and shake for 10 seconds.

5 Use the strainer to pour out the liquid. Make sure to remove all of the water. What's left is butter! Sprinkle salt on it. Try it on a slice of bread!

## WHAT'S GOING ON?

Cream has clumps of fat and **protein**. When they hit each other, they stick together. They form a bigger clump. This big clump is butter.

# FANTASTIC MILK PLASTIC

## WHAT YOU WILL NEED

measuring cups & spoons
saucepan
1 cup whole milk
mixing spoon
glass jar
2 teaspoons white vinegar
strainer
small bowl
small candy mold
dinner knife
waxed paper
Mod Podge
paintbrush
glitter
felt, googly eyes (optional)

# DIRECTIONS PART 1

1. Put the milk in the saucepan. Put the pan on the stove. Turn the heat to low. Stir the milk. Cook for about 15 minutes. Stop when the milk begins to form large lumps.

2. Carefully remove the lumps with a spoon. Put them in the jar.

3. Add the vinegar. Stir for 1 minute. Let the jar sit for 1 hour.

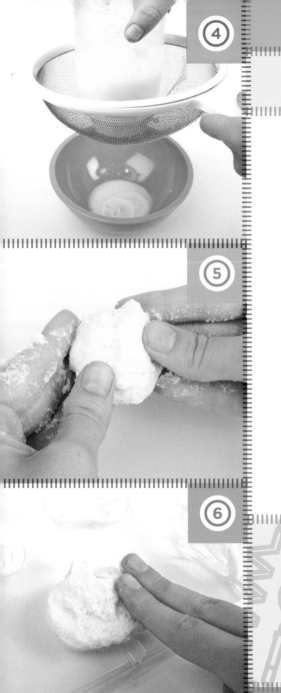

# DIRECTIONS PART 2

④ Hold the strainer over the bowl. Pour the contents of the jar into the strainer.

⑤ Pick up the milk lump. Form it into a solid ball.

⑥ Press the ball into the candy mold. Let it dry for 3 hours.

# DIRECTIONS PART 3

⑦ Gently push a dinner knife into the edges of the mold. Carefully remove the shape. Set it on waxed paper. Let it sit for 3 more hours.

⑧ Brush one side of the shape with Mod Podge.

⑨ Sprinkle glitter on top of the Mod Podge. Let it dry. Then decorate the plastic shape. Add felt or googly eyes.

## WHAT'S GOING ON?

Casein is a **protein** in milk. Vinegar is an **acid**. The acid makes the casein separate from the milk. When the casein hardens, it's a lot like plastic.

# 08

# DISCO DANCING SPAGHETTI

## WHAT YOU WILL NEED

clear drinking glass

water

measuring spoons

3 teaspoons baking soda

food coloring

spoon

10 pieces of uncooked angel hair pasta

5 tablespoons white vinegar

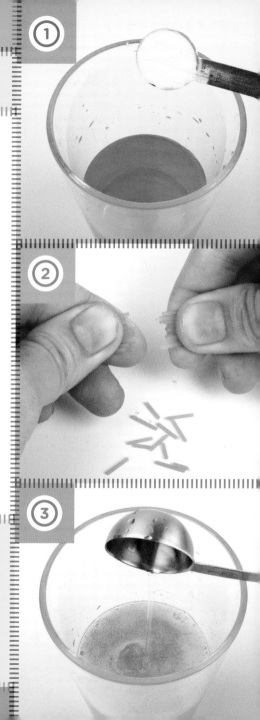

# DIRECTIONS

1. Fill the glass three-fourths full of water. Add the baking soda. Stir in 1 drop of food coloring.

2. Break the pasta into tiny pieces. Put the pieces in the glass.

3. Add the vinegar. Wait a few seconds. The pasta will start to dance. Keep watching for 5 minutes. The dancing might stop and start again!

## WHAT'S GOING ON?

Pasta sinks in water. Adding baking soda and vinegar makes **carbon dioxide** bubbles. The bubbles stick to the pasta. This makes the pasta rise and fall.

# LEMON-POWERED LIGHTBULB

## WHAT YOU WILL NEED

14-gram, coated copper wire

ruler

wire stripper

10 metal alligator clips

pliers

4 lemons

sharp knife

4 pennies

4 large ionized nails

small LED light

# DIRECTIONS PART 1

1   Have an adult help cut 5 pieces of wire. They
    should be about 4 inches (10 cm) long.

②   Have an adult strip ½ inch (1 cm) of coating from
    each end of each piece of wire.

③   Twist the exposed copper ends of all the wires.

④   Put the end of a wire into the back of an alligator
    clip. Use pliers to pinch the back of the clip
    around the wire. Repeat for each end of each
    piece of wire.

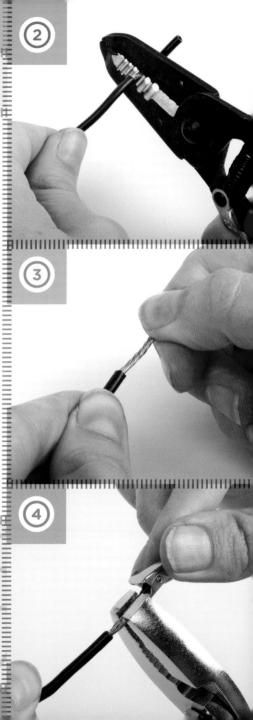

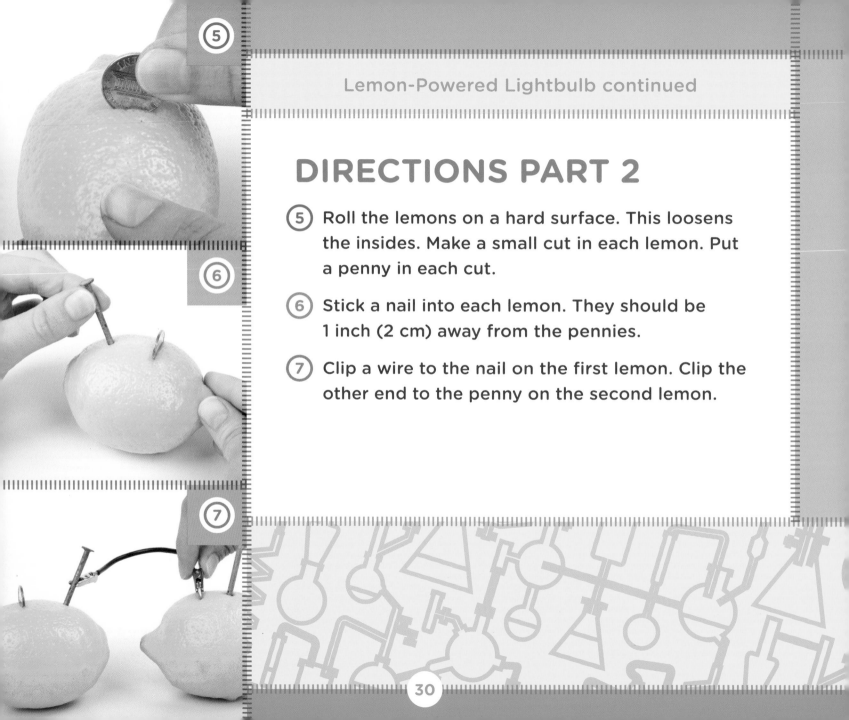

# DIRECTIONS PART 2

⑤ Roll the lemons on a hard surface. This loosens the insides. Make a small cut in each lemon. Put a penny in each cut.

⑥ Stick a nail into each lemon. They should be 1 inch (2 cm) away from the pennies.

⑦ Clip a wire to the nail on the first lemon. Clip the other end to the penny on the second lemon.

# DIRECTIONS PART 3

(8) Connect the third lemon to the second lemon the same way. Then clip the fourth lemon to the third lemon.

(9) Clip the fourth wire to the penny on the first lemon. Clip the fifth wire to the nail on the fourth lemon. The last two wires should each have one unused clip.

(10) Clip one of the unused clips to each of the wires on the LED light. If the light doesn't turn on, switch the clips.

## WHAT'S GOING ON?

Lemon juice has electrolytes. They let electricity flow through the lemons. Connecting pennies and nails that are stuck into lemons creates an electric current. The current lights the LED!

## CONCLUSION

You just found out that science can be super simple! And you did it using food. Keep your thinking cap on! What other experiments can you do with food?

# GLOSSARY

**acid** – a type of chemical that reacts when mixed with a base.

**base** – a type of chemical that reacts when mixed with an acid.

**carbon dioxide** – a gas used to make fizzy, bubbly drinks.

**degree** – the unit used to measure temperature.

**fizzy** – having a lot of tiny hissing bubbles.

**medium** – not the highest or the lowest and not the largest or the smallest.

**neutral** – not an acid or a base.

**protein** – a combination of certain kinds of chemical elements. Proteins are found in all plant and animal cells, such as in meat, eggs, and milk.

**squeeze** – to press or grip something tightly.